# The book belongs to

..........................................

# Top tips!

Welcome to English lingo's vocabulary book for language learners. This note book is designed to help you record and learn new vocabulary in any language. By adding new words every time you study, you will create your own personal dictionary. Here are our top tips for learning vocabulary:

- Write the new word in the left column and the definition in the right column.
- Write the definition in the language you are trying to learn.
- Only use your native language when necessary.
- Test yourself by covering the definitions.
- Don't forget to also try covering the words and guessing them by only looking at the definitions.
- Highlight the words that you find hard to remember.
- Practice making sentences using these highlighted, difficult words.
- When you are reading or listening, pay attention to how the word is used in the sentence. Is it part of a particular phrase or expression?
- Don't forget to record phrasal verbs, collocations and other expressions.
- Make a note of what kind of word it is. You can use a simple system, for example write (v) for a verb and (n) for a noun.

F

F

F

G

# I

I

| | | K |
|---|---|---|
| kultur | culture | |
| kulturer | cultures | |
| konferenser | conferences | |
| kommittén | the comittee | |
| kommitté | a —"— | |

5

5

5

5

T

T

U

V

V

# V

Printed in Great Britain
by Amazon